PREPARING FOR

CHRIST'S RETURN

BY

CHARLES F. STANLEY

THOMAS NELSON
Since 1798

Published in Nashville, Tennessee, by Thomas Nelson, Inc., and distributed in
Canada by Word Communications, Ltd., Richmond, British Columbia.

G$_C$B

Editing, layout, and design by Gregory C. Benoit Publishing, Old Mystic, CT

Unless otherwise noted, Scripture quotations are from the New King James Version.
© 1982 by Thomas Nelson, Inc. Used by permission. All rights reserved.

The Bible version used in this publication is The New King James Version. Copyright
1979, 1980, 1982, Thomas Nelson, Inc., Publishers.

ISBN 1-4185-4118-4

Printed in the United States of America

09 10 11 12 13 RRD 5 4 3 2 1

Contents

Preparing for His Return

So many books have been written about the coming of the Lord that much confusion about His return exists today. Much of what has been written relates to timetables of events, with some authors predicting when the Lord will return, some attempting to explain certain world events in light of biblical prophecy, and some arguing against the physical return of the Lord Jesus Christ. Rather than attempting to predict God's timeline for Jesus' return, this study guide will focus on what the Bible says about several key events related to Christ's return, about God's overall plan for mankind, and about what God desires from us in the way of preparation for His return.

The Bible must be our foremost source on this topic. It is the reference to which we must return continually if we are to have a sound understanding about what lies ahead for the church and for the world.

This book does not try to discern precisely when the Lord is coming. Instead, it encourages us to live in a constant state of readiness for His appearing and helps us prepare for His return. It also helps us prepare others for His coming. This study book teaches only on those things about which we can be certain, focusing on Bible truth rather than man's interpretation of end-time events.

This book can be used by you alone or by several people in a small-group study. At various times, you will be asked to relate to the material in one of these four ways:

1. *What new insights have you gained?* Make notes about the insights that you have. You may want to record them in your Bible or in a sepa-

rate journal. As you reflect back over your insights, you are likely to see how God has moved in your life.

2. *Have you ever had a similar experience?* Each of us approaches the Bible from a unique background—our own particular set of relationships and experiences. Our experiences do not make the Bible true—the Word of God is truth regardless of our opinion about it. It is important, however, to share our experiences in order to see how God's truth can be applied to human lives.

3. *How do you feel about the material presented?* Emotional responses do not give validity to the Scriptures, nor should we trust our emotions as a gauge for our faith. In small-group Bible study, however, it is good for participants to express their emotions. The Holy Spirit often communicates with us through this unspoken language.

4. *In what way do you feel challenged to respond or to act?* God's Word may cause you to feel inspired or challenged to change something in your life. Take the challenge seriously and find ways of acting upon it. If God reveals to you a particular need that He wants *you* to address, take that as "marching orders" from God. God is expecting you to *do* something with the challenge that He has just given you.

Start and conclude your Bible study sessions in prayer. Ask God to give you spiritual eyes to see and spiritual ears to hear. As you conclude your study, ask the Lord to seal what you have learned so that you will never forget it. Ask Him to help you grow into the fullness of the stature of Christ Jesus.

Again, I caution you to keep the Bible at the center of your study. A genuine Bible study stays focused on God's Word and promotes a growing faith and a closer walk with the Holy Spirit in *each* person who participates.

Lesson 1

Christ Is Coming Again!

☙ In This Lesson ☞

Learning: What does it mean that Jesus is coming back to earth?

Growing: What difference does it make in my life today?

If you have accepted Jesus Christ as your Savior, I have great news for you today: Jesus is coming to earth again! If you have not accepted Jesus Christ as your Savior, I have very sobering news for you: Jesus is coming to earth again.

For the Christian, the return of Jesus is great and glorious news. It marks the fulfillment of our life and purpose on earth. It signals the most joyous moment of our existence: the moment when we see Jesus face to face and are restored to our loved ones who have died in Christ. His return will be the most exciting, exhilarating experience of our lives.

For those who do not believe in Jesus, the return of the Lord will be a terrible and fearful event. The "Day of the Lord" is described in horrific and catastrophic terms in the Scriptures. Christ's return is not a day of joy for those who have not accepted Him as their Savior and Lord.

Living in Eager Anticipation

The early church lived in eager anticipation of Christ's return. These earlier believers included those who had been close followers of Jesus or who had seen and heard Him. They knew how wonderful it was to be with Jesus, and they were eager to be in His immediate presence again. Others in the early church had had contact with Jesus' disciples and followers. They had heard the apostles and others speak of being with Jesus, and they could hardly wait for their turn to be in His presence. There was great enthusiasm in the early church for Christ's return, and His return was frequently the topic of the believers' conversations. The same attitude should be found in believers today: we are to be just as eager and enthusiastic as the early church. With every day that passes we are one day closer to Christ's return. In fact, He may come today!

The subject of Christ's return regularly elicits certain negative responses in those who believe the Gospel. First, there are those who doubt that He is coming. They take the approach that it's been so many years since He walked on earth, and perhaps we have the wrong understanding. Perhaps He isn't coming after all. Perhaps we have misinterpreted what Jesus said or what the Bible means on this subject. But Christ *is* coming again. The Bible means what it says, and it is very clear on the matter. Furthermore, God is always faithful to His Word. He does what He promises to do. You can count on Christ's return with just as much assurance as you can count on all of God's other promises.

Second, there are those who fear Christ's return. They wonder if they are prepared for it. They are concerned that Christ's return may affect them in a negative way. Let me assure you today: if you have accepted Christ Jesus as your Savior and are seeking daily to follow and serve Him as your Lord, you have nothing to fear. His return will be the most wonderful moment of your life.

Still others are fearful on behalf of their loved ones, especially those who do not yet know Jesus as Savior. They have reason to be concerned. Now, more than ever, is the time for us to share very directly and openly with those we love, explaining how important it is that they believe in Jesus and accept His death on the cross as the atoning sacrifice for their sins. Today is the day for salvation (Heb. 3:12–15).

The Benefits to Those Who Look for His Coming

An eager anticipation of the Lord's return produces four tremendous qualities in us as believers:

1. An urgency for souls. A keen awareness of the coming of the Lord creates a desire to do all we can to reach lost souls now with the message of salvation.

2. A priority on eternal reward. When we are eagerly anticipating the Lord's return, we are much more focused on doing things that count for eternity. We simply do not have the time to waste on things that are frivolous or temporal. Our focus is on complete obedience to what the Lord is calling us to do today.

3. A purity of heart. The return of Christ calls us to examine our hearts and to repent of those things that we know are displeasing to the Lord.

4. An exceedingly great joy and hope. The return of Christ brings hope to the heart, a song of joy to the soul. When we are with Christ, we will experience no more sorrow, sickness, pain, or loneliness. We will enter into everlasting perfection and experience beauty, holiness, and wholeness beyond our imagination.

"But what if Christ doesn't come in my lifetime?" you may ask. The truth is, if you are living in eager anticipation of the Lord's return, the benefits of expecting Him are the same. If you live an entire lifetime with an urgency to see lost souls saved, a focus on those things that are of eternal benefit, a purity of heart, and great joy and hope—what a life that is! It is a life of genuine purpose, satisfaction, and meaning—and it is a life that will bring great reward in eternity. Can there be any better way to live?

> Then they will see the Son of Man coming in the clouds with great power and glory. And then He will send His angels, and gather together His elect from the four winds, from the farthest part of earth to the farthest part of heaven.
>
> —Mark 13:26–27

How often do you think about Christ's return? Do you honestly believe that it might happen soon, or do you tend to assume that it won't be for a long time yet?

Have you accepted Jesus as your Savior? If not, what is preventing you from doing so right now?

Why does the return of Christ matter to Christians? To non-Christians?

Today and Tomorrow

TODAY: GOD HAS PROMISED THAT JESUS WILL RETURN TO EARTH, AND HE ALWAYS KEEPS HIS PROMISES.

TOMORROW: I WILL BEGIN TO LIVE IN THE ANTICIPATION THAT JESUS MIGHT RETURN THIS VERY DAY.

∽ Notes and Prayer Requests: ∽

LESSON 2

The Promise of His Return

───────── ❧ In This Lesson ☙ ─────────

LEARNING: WHAT WILL HAPPEN AFTER CHRIST RETURNS?

GROWING: HOW SHOULD I BE PREPARING FOR THAT DAY?

❧

The Lord Jesus Christ has promised that He will return. We find certainty of His promise in Scripture. There are several terms that are important for us to clarify as we begin this study:

Rapture. This refers to a "catching away" of the church prior to the Lord's return. The word *rapture* does not occur in the New Testament, but it is the word that has been used traditionally by the church from the earliest sermons and commentaries written by Christians. The Rapture is a time when all believers are united with the Lord Jesus Christ prior to His coming again to rule and reign on the earth.

Second Coming and Millennium. The first coming of Christ was when Jesus, the only begotten Son of God, was born as a baby in Bethlehem. Jesus, a real person in a real body, walked the earth to preach a vibrant message of God's love and forgiveness, to heal and deliver all who came to Him for healing and deliverance, and to die a sacrificial death of atonement on the cross so that mankind could be reconciled fully to God the Father.

The second coming of Christ refers to the time when Jesus will return again to the earth, this time as the King of kings and Lord of lords. He will reside on earth in a physical, glorified form, this time to rule and reign over all mankind and all creation. Those who are believers in Christ Jesus will rule and reign with Him.

The reign of Christ on the earth has been described in Revelation 20:6: they "shall reign with Him a thousand years." The Millennium, a thousand-year period, has been the subject of much debate through the centuries, but of this we can be certain: it is a time when Satan will be bound, Christ will be in charge, and the peace that has eluded mankind will prevail.

The Day of the Lord and the Great Tribulation. The term *Day of the Lord* is used primarily in the Old Testament, and it refers to a day of great judgment on the earth—a day when the wrath of God is poured out on the earth by fire, the earth is purged of all sin, and all who reside on earth are in total subjugation to an awesome display of the Lord's power.

In Christianity the Day of the Lord has been linked to the Great Tribulation, which is not regarded as an actual *day* but rather a seven-year period of great distress and turmoil. It is a time that ends with the Battle of Armageddon and the return of Jesus to rule and reign on the earth.

Numerous Scriptures refer to one or more of these events. We will be able to focus on only a limited number of them in this study. Our purpose in this first lesson is to see what Jesus said about His return and about how we are to prepare ourselves. On the night before His crucifixion, Jesus said to His disciples:

"Now the Son of Man is glorified, and God is glorified in Him.
If God is glorified in Him, God will also glorify Him in Himself,

and glorify Him immediately. Little children, I shall be with you a little while longer. You will seek Me; and as I said to the Jews, 'Where I am going, you cannot come,' so now I say to you. A new commandment I give to you, that you love one another; as I have loved you, that you also love one another. By this all will know that you are My disciples, if you have love for one another."

—John 13:31–35

❧ Why did Jesus stress the need for His disciples to love one another? What does loving others have to do with preparing for His return?

❧ How did God glorify Jesus in His death and resurrection? How will God be glorified by Christ's return to earth?

Jesus was referring to His death by crucifixion and to the three days that He would be away from the disciples (the time between His crucifixion and resurrection). Note that Jesus was most concerned that during this time of His absence, the disciples would "love one another."

Simon Peter asked the Lord after He had made this statement, "Lord, where are You going?" Jesus replied, "Where I am going you cannot follow Me now, but you shall follow Me afterward" (John 13:36). Jesus was again referring to His death. This was not the time for Peter to die, but at the same time Jesus noted that one day Peter would die a similar death.

Peter again said, "Lord, why can I not follow You now? I will lay down my life for Your sake." Jesus answered Peter, "Will you lay down your life for My sake? Most assuredly, I say to you, the rooster shall not crow till you have denied Me three times" (John 13:37–38). Then, after addressing Peter's boast, Jesus addressed Peter's deep concern and grief. He said:

Let not your heart be troubled; you believe in God, believe also in Me. In My Father's house are many mansions; if it were not so, I would have told you. I go to prepare a place for you. And if I go and prepare a place for you, I will come again and receive you to Myself; that where I am, there you may be also. And where I go you know, and the way you know.

—John 14:1–4

❧ Why did Jesus command His disciples not to let their hearts be troubled? Why was this a command and not merely a suggestion?

❧ How can fear and anxiety cloud our thinking about Christ's imminent return? How can such fears be overcome?

I want you to note five specific things that Jesus said to Peter and His other disciples about this time that He would be away:

1. "Don't let My absence trouble you. Don't worry or be in anguish about My absence."

2. "Believe in Me." In other words, "Trust Me. Recognize that God's plan is unfolding right on schedule."

3. "I am going to prepare a place for you."

4. "I am coming back for you so that you can always be with Me."

5. "You know deep within yourself both where I am going and what it will take for you to be with Me."

These are the same things the Lord says to us today in His absence:

➤ "Don't be worried by the fact that you can't see Me or that I am away from you."

➤ "Continue to believe in Me. All things are unfolding just as God our heavenly Father has planned them."

The Lord is preparing a place for us—and what a wonderful place it's going to be! He is going to return and receive us to Himself so that we will never be separated from Him again. We know this will happen, we know where we will one day be, and we know it with certainty because we know how to ensure our relationship with Jesus Christ forever.

Thomas, another of Jesus' disciples, said, "Lord, we do not know where You are going, and how can we know the way?" Jesus replied to Thomas, "I am the way, the truth, and the life. No one comes to the Father except through Me" (John 14:5–6). As believers in Christ Jesus, we can have great confidence in these words of our Lord. He is the way to salvation, He is the full embodiment of God's plan and purpose for mankind, and He is life everlasting.

When we accept Jesus as our Savior, we receive God's forgiveness and the Holy Spirit, whom Jesus sends to indwell all who believe in Him. In receiving Jesus we receive the One who is the way, the truth, and the life. We know the way because we know Christ as our Savior. We know the truth because we have the Holy Spirit within us to convict and convince us of the truth. We know life because the Holy Spirit is eternal and He resides in us; we will live forever because we live in Him and He lives in us.

That is our assurance as we await the Lord's coming. We are going to be with Him forever, regardless of the events that occur between this very moment and the moment that we see Christ face to face. If we are alive at the time of the Rapture, we will immediately be with Him. If we die before the Rapture, we will instantly be with the Lord when we die. We will dwell in the place the Lord has prepared for us.

> Behold, I tell you a mystery: We shall not all sleep, but we shall all be changed—in a moment, in the twinkling of an eye, at the last trumpet. For the trumpet will sound, and the dead will be raised incorruptible, and we shall be changed.
>
> —1 Corinthians 15:51–52

❧ What does it mean to "be raised incorruptible"? How will our lives be different when we are incorruptible?

❧ What does it mean that "we shall not all sleep"? What does this teach about Christ's return?

The Uninterrupted Reign of our Lord

One of the most wonderful passages in the Scriptures encompasses both Christ's first and second coming:

> For unto us a Child is born,
> Unto us a Son is given;
> And the government will be upon His shoulder.
> And His name will be called
> Wonderful, Counselor, Mighty God,
> Everlasting Father, Prince of Peace.
> Of the increase of His government and peace
> There will be no end,
> Upon the throne of David and over His kingdom,
> To order it and establish it with judgment and justice
> From that time forward, even forever.
> The zeal of the Lord of hosts will perform this.

—Isaiah 9:6–7

This passage refers to an important concept related to the Lord's return: We are all subject to the Lord's rule. Not all people on the earth have accepted that fact; not all acknowledge Jesus as Savior and Lord. Nonetheless, from the moment Jesus was born, He instituted active rule over this world. No powers of darkness could prevail over Him during His earthly life, and no powers of darkness can prevail over Him now or ever. The uninterrupted reign of Jesus has already begun! Jesus sits at the right hand of God the Father today to order and establish His kingdom "with judgment and justice." His will is being done on earth even now, regardless of our ability to recognize it.

What we also see in this passage is the truth that the "increase of His government and peace" will continue with "no end." The Lord Jesus is not losing power the longer He delays His return to the earth. He is increasing His authority over the earth. With every sinner who comes to Him, Jesus increases His government and peace. With every victory over the enemy, the Lord extends His justice and righteousness. The rule of the Lord will continue without interruption until the day when we are all with Him. And what a great and glorious day that will be!

☞ Put each of the Lord's names from Isaiah 9 in your own words:

Wonderful:

Counselor:

Mighty God:

Everlasting Father:

Prince of Peace:

Our Agenda as Believers

As Jesus was preparing to ascend to the Father, He told His disciples to stay in Jerusalem to await the coming of the Promise of the Father, the Holy Spirit. He said, "You have heard from Me; for John truly baptized with water, but you shall be baptized with the Holy Spirit not many days from now" (Acts 1:4–5). The disciples asked Him, "Lord, will You at this time restore the kingdom to Israel?" (Acts 1:6) Read closely what Jesus said to them:

> It is not for you to know times or seasons which the Father has put in His own authority. But you shall receive power when the Holy Spirit has come upon you; and you shall be witnesses to Me in Jerusalem, and in all Judea and Samaria, and to the end of the earth.

> —Acts 1:7–8

Jesus made it very clear what we as believers are to be doing until He returns and receives us to Himself:

We are to receive the power of the Holy Spirit into our lives. We are to yield ourselves daily to the Holy Spirit, asking Him to direct our steps into God's perfect will for our lives.

We are to be His witnesses "to the end of the earth." We are to share the Gospel of Jesus Christ with every person possible prior to the Lord's return or our death, whichever comes first.

The Literal Return of Christ

Jesus was taken up and a cloud received Him out of the sight of the disciples who were gathered with Him on the Mount of Olives. The Bible tells us that "two men stood by them in white apparel, who also said, 'Men of Galilee, why do you stand gazing up into heaven? This same Jesus, who was taken up from you into heaven, will so come in like manner as you saw Him go into heaven'" (Acts 1:10–11).

Jesus will return in the same manner that He departed. His ascension was literal; His return will be literal. His ascension was in bodily form; His return will be in bodily form.

The second coming of the Lord will not be a coming in "spirit" or a coming in "idea" or a coming in "miracles"—it will be a real coming, just as His ascension was a real going.

> Behold, He is coming with clouds, and every eye will see Him, even they who pierced Him. And all the tribes of the earth will mourn because of Him.
>
> —Revelation 1:7

Who are the "tribes of the earth"? Why will they mourn when Christ returns?

Why will Jesus show Himself to everyone on earth, including those who have rejected Him?

Yes, the Lord is coming again! We must ask ourselves these questions: Am I doing the things the Lord has told me to do until that day? Am I doing all I can to be ready for His return?

❧ Today and Tomorrow ❧

TODAY: JESUS WILL LITERALLY RETURN TO EARTH IN BODILY FORM AND THE ENTIRE WORLD WILL SEE HIM.

TOMORROW: I WILL ASK THE LORD TO SHOW ME WHAT HE WANTS ME TO DO IN PREPARATION FOR THAT DAY.

❧ Notes and Prayer Requests: ❧

LESSON 3

God's Magnificent Master Plan

---------- ❦ **In This Lesson** ❦ ----------

LEARNING: WHAT SIGNS WILL GOD GIVE PRIOR TO CHRIST'S RETURN?

GROWING: WILL GOD'S PEOPLE BE IN DANGER IN THAT DAY?

God has a magnificent master plan for His creation. It is a plan that has been in place since the beginning of time. It is a plan that is unfolding just as God intended it to unfold. One of the most beneficial ways for us to consider the second coming of Christ is by looking at His first coming. We see in the first coming an amazing series of events and prophecies woven together in precision and culminating in the birth of Jesus. The Lord prepared the world for the birth of Jesus in four main ways:

1. Spoken prophecies

2. Symbols and prophetic signs

3. Sovereign provision for and preparation of His people

4. Sovereign rule over nations and nature

As He prepared the world for the first coming, so He will prepare the world for the Second Coming.

Proclamations of the Prophets

God spoke repeatedly through His prophets about the coming of the Messiah, Jesus Christ, His only begotten Son. The first prophecy is often overlooked, but it has bearing on the second coming of the Lord. It was a word of the Lord to the serpent that deceived Eve:

> And I will put enmity
> Between you and the woman,
> And between your seed and her Seed;
> He shall bruise your head,
> And you shall bruise His heel.

—Genesis 3:15

Eve's Seed was Jesus, her heir. Satan was allowed to "bruise" the heel of Jesus, a bruising that was an annoyance. Jesus, in contrast, will bruise Satan's head, utterly destroying his power, authority, and influence. The bruise to the head of Satan will mean a total defeat.

We must never lose sight of the fact that Jesus came to destroy the works of the devil. He came to win back what the devil tried to steal from God. He came back to defeat the devil at every turn. What Jesus began at the Cross, He continues to do by the power of His Holy Spirit in human lives today. The work of Jesus in defeating the devil is ongoing.

The purpose of Christ's coming as our Savior was to destroy the devil's authority and power over our spirits, souls, and bodies; Jesus came to restore man to God. In His second coming Christ will restore all of creation and all of the world's systems to God in both the spiritual and natural realms.

☙ Read Genesis 3:1–19. What were the specific details of God's curse on Adam? On Eve? On Satan?

☙ In what sense did Satan bruise the heel of Jesus? In what ways will God crush the devil's head when Christ returns?

A number of other prophecies in the Old Testament refer to the specifics of Christ's birth, life, and death. Through the ages our heavenly Father made known His plans for the birth of His Son. The Lord is no less precise in His plans and preparation for the second coming of Christ. Following are three prophecies related to Christ's birth, and three related to His return. The prophecies related to Christ's birth have been fulfilled with precision, so we can expect the prophecies related to Christ's return also to be fulfilled in detail.

> But you, Bethlehem Ephrathah, though you are little among the thousands of Judah, yet out of you shall come forth to Me the One to be Ruler in Israel, whose goings forth are from of old, from everlasting.
>
> —Micah 5:2

How was this prophecy fulfilled in the life of Christ?

Rejoice greatly, O daughter of Zion! Shout, O daughter of Jerusalem! Behold, your King is coming to you; He is just and having salvation, lowly and riding on a donkey, a colt, the foal of a donkey.

—Zechariah 9:9

How was this prophecy fulfilled in the life of Christ?

Therefore the Lord Himself will give you a sign: Behold, the virgin shall conceive and bear a Son, and shall call His name Immanuel.

—Isaiah 7:14

How was this prophecy fulfilled in the life of Christ?

Now the Spirit expressly says that in latter times some will depart from the faith, giving heed to deceiving spirits and doctrines of demons, speaking lies in hypocrisy, having their own conscience seared with a hot iron, forbidding to marry, and commanding to abstain from foods which God created to be received with thanksgiving by those who believe and know the truth.

—1 Timothy 4:1–3

What signs will precede Christ's return, according to these verses?

But know this, that in the last days perilous times will come: For men will be lovers of themselves, lovers of money, boasters, proud, blasphemers, disobedient to parents, unthankful, unholy, unloving, unforgiving, slanderers, without self-control, brutal, despisers of good, traitors, headstrong, haughty, lovers of pleasure rather than lovers of God, having a form of godliness but denying its power. And from such people turn away!

—2 Timothy 3:1–5

What signs will precede Christ's return, according to these verses?

For the time will come when they will not endure sound doc-
trine, but according to their own desires, because they have
itching ears, they will heap up for themselves teachers; and
they will turn their ears away from the truth, and be turned
aside to fables. But you be watchful in all things, endure afflic-
tions, do the work of an evangelist, fulfill your ministry.

—2 Timothy 4:3–5

🐟 What signs will precede Christ's return, according to these
verses?

Symbols and Prophetic Signs

One of the ways in which the Lord foretold the coming of Jesus and the
nature of the Messiah was through signs and symbols. One of the foremost symbols is that of the shed blood of a lamb. Throughout the Old
Testament we find the shedding of the blood of a lamb to be associated
with the forgiveness of sins. In the Garden of Eden God covered Adam
and Eve with animal skins, and the implication is that an innocent animal was slain by God to provide a covering for Adam and Eve, a covering that reminded them continually of the fact that their sin would result in a physical death. Later, God instituted animal sacrifices for the
remission of sin and as a "blood covering" against death (especially at
Passover and the Day of Atonement). The necessity for blood sacrifices
ended with the blood sacrifice of Jesus on the cross.

Another sign that was used in a prophetic way by God was the crossing of the Red Sea. The passage of God's people through the water was a sign of baptism to come. The pillar of cloud by day and of fire by night that led the Israelites through the wilderness was a prophetic sign that God would send His Spirit to lead His people to the fulfillment of all His promises.

It is important to recognize that the people to whom these signs were given did not understand their full importance. The signs were recognized by them as acts of deliverance, healing, and help. Similarly, we may not understand the full significance of the signs prophesied in the New Testament about the coming of the Lord. They can be understood by us, however, in the same way that the signs of old were understood: we will perceive them as signs of the Lord's deliverance, healing, and help.

One of the signs Jesus gave as an indicator of His coming and the end of the age is described in Matthew 24:4–8:

"Take heed that no one deceives you. For many will come in My name, saying, 'I am the Christ,' and will deceive many. And you will hear of wars and rumors of wars. See that you are not troubled; for all these things must come to pass, but the end is not yet. For nation will rise against nation, and kingdom against kingdom. And there will be famines, pestilences, and earthquakes in various places. All these are the beginning of sorrows."

—Matthew 24:4–8

⚘ What specific signs did Jesus refer to in the preceding passage? Are there examples of any in the world today?

⚘ What commands does the Lord give to His people in responding to these signs? How should Christians respond when such things take place?

Sovereign Provision for and Protection of God's People

We find countless stories in the Old Testament that, taken together, reveal God's divine protection and provision for His elect. God's people were sovereignly guided, spared, guarded, and nurtured as part of God's plan to teach and prepare His people for the Messiah. He worked as a Great Shepherd, guiding His sheep across arid ground and dangerous ravines until He brought them to a place of green pastures and still waters.

Slowly over time, bit by bit, the Lord revealed Himself to His people. He imparted facets of His name as He revealed His character. He performed miracles and issued specific prophecies to reveal His purposes. As you read through some of the names of God below, consider the many ways in which God revealed Himself to the Israelites as a means of teaching them about Himself and as a means of preparing them for Jesus.

Name	Meaning
Abba	Father
Shaddai	Almighty
El Olam	Everlasting God
Elohim	Creator
El Roi	The One who responds to need
Qedosh Yisrael	The Holy God, set apart for Israel
Adonai	Master, Lord
YHWH	Personal Lord
YHWH-Nissi	The Lord who protects me
YHWH-Sabaoth	The Lord of hosts (armies)
YHWH-Shalom	The Lord of peace
YHWH-Yireh	The Lord who provides
YHWH-Tsidkenu	The righteous Lord
YHWH-Rohi	The Lord who is the Shepherd of loving care

Now consider some of the names that have been given to Jesus. How do they prepare us and teach us about the Lord's nature and character—not only now but in His coming again?

Name	Meaning
Alpha and Omega	Beginning and Ending
Bread of Life	Essential for life
Chief Cornerstone	The sure foundation
High Priest	Our mediator
Immanuel	"God with us"—the One who always stands with us
Jesus	Yahweh saves
King of kings, Lord of lords	The sovereign almighty
Lamb of God	The One who offers His life as a sacrifice for sin
Rabbi	Teacher
Shepherd	The One who gives guidance and protection
Word	God's supreme communication to mankind

Take time to pray right now, praising God for the elements of His character described in these names.

Sovereign Rule of Nations and Nature

The Lord governs His people and prepares them for the fulfillment of His plan and purposes, and He also governs all nations and all of nature. Many Bible scholars refer to the four-hundred-year span between Malachi and Matthew as the "silent years." God was anything but inactive during this time. It was during these four hundred years that Alexander the Great conquered the nations around the Mediterranean and united the world under the Greek language. It was during this period that the Greek Bible was written (Septuagint), which was a great force in the evangelism of the Gentile world after the crucifixion of Jesus.

God used the Romans to build good roads, institute free and open travel, and allow the coexistence of many religions—all of which were factors that enhanced the spread of the gospel during the first century. It was a Roman census that brought Joseph and Mary to Bethlehem for the birth of Jesus, in fulfillment of prophecy. It was Roman crucifixion that provided the means for Christ's death as one "lifted up" for the salvation of mankind. On the night that Jesus was born, God arranged for a new star to appear in the heavens, a star that was a signal to the wise men to bring their gifts that would honor Jesus as our Messiah (prophet, priest, and king).

Throughout the ages, God was doing His great and mighty work. If God could so arrange the history of the nations and the course of nature in anticipation of the birth of Jesus, surely He is at work arranging the history of nations and the course of nature in anticipation of Christ's return.

God's preparation is meticulous. He leaves no detail unfinished. His plan for mankind through the ages is unfolding just as He designed it to unfold. There are no surprises, no detours, no delays. We can trust God's plan. We can trust God's promises regarding His people and the Lord's return. He is utterly faithful to His Word and to those who believe it.

In the beginning was the Word, and the Word was with God, and the Word was God. He was in the beginning with God. All things were made through Him, and without Him nothing was made that was made.

—John 1:1–3

Who is "the Word" described in these verses? What do these verses reveal about Him?

Read Genesis 1. What role did "the Word" have in creation? What does this suggest about God's power to mold creation to suit His purposes?

❧ Today and Tomorrow ❧

TODAY: GOD HAS ABSOLUTE CONTROL OVER ALL CREATION, INCLUDING CURRENT WORLD EVENTS.

TOMORROW: I WILL SPEND TIME THIS WEEK MEDITATING ON THE NAMES OF GOD.

❧ Notes and Prayer Requests: ❧

Lesson 4

In the Fullness of Time

The question most people ask about the second coming of Christ is this: "When will it be?" Jesus' own disciples asked this question of the Lord. They said to Jesus privately, "Tell us, when will these things be?" (Matt. 24:3). Jesus gave them several general signs that would indicate that the time was approaching, but then He said this:

> Of that day and hour no one knows, not even the angels of heaven, but My Father only. But as the days of Noah were, so also will the coming of the Son of Man be. For as in the days before the flood, they were eating and drinking, marrying and giving in marriage, until the day that Noah entered the ark, and did not know until the flood came and took them all away, so also will the coming of the Son of Man be ... Watch therefore, for you do not know what hour your Lord is coming.
>
> —Matthew 24:36–39, 42

Read Genesis 6. What was the world like in the days of Noah? What signs will be apparent prior to Christ's return, according to the verses above?

Why does no one know the day and hour of Christ's return? What does this suggest about those who claim to know when it will happen?

No matter what any person may calculate from the Scriptures, we will not know the day and hour of Christ's coming. Only the Father has that information. There are several things, however, of which we can be certain, and it is on those things that we will focus in this lesson.

God's Timing Is Perfect

God did not send Jesus to the earth the first time without preparation that included an absolute perfection in timing. Neither will Jesus return to the earth without preparation and perfect timing. The fact is, however, that God's timing is not always our timing. God's ways are not our ways. As we read in Isaiah:

> "My thoughts are not your thoughts,
> Nor are your ways My ways," says the Lord.
> "For as the heavens are higher than the earth,
> So are My ways higher than your ways,
> And My thoughts than your thoughts."

> —Isaiah 55:8–9

What we count on is that God will send His Son back to earth in the perfection of His timing, not necessarily in the timing we desire. One of the concepts that we find repeatedly in the Scriptures is the "fullness of time." Paul wrote to the Galatians that God sent Jesus to the earth as our Savior in "the fullness of the time" (Gal. 4:4). The fullness of the time refers to the perfection of timing. All things are in place; all prerequisites have been completed; all things are ready.

A normal, healthy baby is not born according to a calendar or a physician's predictions but in the fullness of time, the right time for that baby to be born. God sees things from a perspective of eternity. He is not locked into time as we are. He sees precisely the right moment when all things are in place according to His plan, and in that moment He acts. The apostle Paul wrote to Timothy, "Keep this commandment without spot, blameless until our Lord Jesus Christ's appearing, which He will manifest in His own time, He who is the blessed and only Potentate, the King of kings and Lord of lords, who alone has immortality, dwelling in unapproachable light" (1 Tim. 6:14–16). Jesus will return when the time is right according to God the Father.

> But when the fullness of the time had come, God sent forth His Son, born of a woman, born under the law, to redeem those who were under the law, that we might receive the adoption as sons.
>
> —Galatians 4:4–5

≈ What things needed to be completed before "the fullness of time had come" for Christ's birth?

≈ What things will need to be completed before Christ's return?

The Character of the End Times

If we cannot know the precise timing of the Lord's return, what *can* we know about God's timing? We can know with certainty three things related to timing: we will be able to discern the signs associated with the coming of the Lord as they happen; we will have a sense that the time is drawing close; and we are to be ready at all times. We will deal with the first of these three signs in this lesson and the remaining two in the next lesson.

∞ Discerning the Signs as They Happen ∞

We will have an understanding of end-time events as they happen. Many people desire to predict future events in the light of current events, but this is not the pattern given to us in the Scriptures. Rather, we will have an understanding of events as they occur. Jesus said to the Pharisees who asked Him to show them a sign from heaven:

> When it is evening you say, "It will be fair weather, for the sky is red"; and in the morning, "It will be foul weather today, for the sky is red and threatening." Hypocrites! You know how to discern the face of the sky, but you cannot discern the signs of the times. A wicked and adulterous generation seeks after a sign, and no sign shall be given to it except the sign of the prophet Jonah.

> —Matthew 16:2–4

❧ Why did Jesus call the Pharisees hypocrites? In what way were they being hypocritical?

❧ What signs do you use to predict the weather? What signs does Scripture give of Christ's return?

Jesus was referring to the signs surrounding His death and resurrection. Jonah spent three days in the belly of a fish (Jonah 1–2), which the Lord pointed to as a sign of His own death and resurrection—but that sign was not understood until after the resurrection. There were many things that Jesus said and did that His closest disciples did not understand until after Jesus was crucified and risen from the dead. John wrote this about the fulfillment of the prophecy concerning Jesus riding into Jerusalem on a donkey's colt: "His disciples did not understand these things at first; but when Jesus was glorified, then they remembered that these things were written about Him and that they had done these things to Him" (John 12:16).

As noted in Matthew 16:4: "A wicked and adulterous generation seeks after a sign, and no sign shall be given to it." The world will not be able to discern the spiritual signs of God at work. That was true then; it is true now. We must have spiritual eyes and spiritual ears in order to discern spiritual matters. Discernment is the function of the Holy Spirit in our lives. In Matthew 24, Jesus began His explanation of future events in this way:

> Take heed that no one deceives you. For many will come in My name, saying, "I am the Christ," and will deceive many. And you will hear of wars and rumors of wars. See that you are not troubled; for all these things must come to pass, but the end is not yet. For nation will rise against nation, and kingdom against kingdom. And there will be famines, pestilences, and earthquakes in various places. All these are the beginning of sorrows. Then they will deliver you up to tribulation and kill you, and you will be hated by all nations for My name's sake. And then many will be offended, will betray one another, and will hate one another. Then many false prophets will rise up and deceive many. And because lawlessness will abound, the love of many will grow cold. But he who endures to the end shall be saved. And this gospel of the kingdom will be preached in all the world as a witness to all the nations, and then the end will come.

> —Matthew 24:4–14

We included part of this passage in a previous lesson, but I want to point out four things that are very important as we await the coming of Christ:

43

First, Jesus warned against deception. He said, "Take heed that no one deceives you." Deceit is a subtle form of lying; it is twisting the truth so that it is nearly impossible to tell the truth from a lie. As believers in Christ, we are always to stand against deceit and be quick to speak the Bible's truth.

> So the great dragon was cast out, that serpent of old, called the Devil and Satan, who deceives the whole world; he was cast to the earth, and his angels were cast out with him.

> —Revelation 12:9

Why is Satan called "that serpent of old"? How does this relate to Genesis 3?

How does Satan deceive the world today? Give some specific examples.

Second, Jesus foretold a time of great confusion—a time of offense, betrayal, hatred, false prophets, and lawlessness. As believers in Christ, we are to display the very opposite traits: loyalty to Christ and to other believers, love, truthful teaching, and law-abiding behavior. We are to be agents of peace.

> For where envy and self-seeking exist, confusion and every evil thing are there. But the wisdom that is from above is first pure, then peaceable, gentle, willing to yield, full of mercy and good fruits, without partiality and without hypocrisy.
>
> —James 3:16–17

Define these qualities in your own words, giving examples of each:

Pure:

Peaceable:

Willing to yield:

Without partiality:

Third, Jesus called for endurance. He said, "He who endures to the end shall be saved." We are to persevere in what we know to be true and in those works that we know to be righteous.

> Blessed is the man who endures temptation; for when he has been approved, he will receive the crown of life which the Lord has promised to those who love Him.

> —James 1:12

🙋 What is the "crown of life"? Why is it a result of enduring temptation?

🙋 Why does James say that we are to endure temptation rather than resist it? What is the difference? How is each done?

Fourth, Jesus spoke of the gospel being preached in all the world as a witness to all nations. We are to share the gospel with as many people as possible, individually in our personal witness and joining with others to reach those in far away places who still have not heard about Jesus.

Each of these four things calls us to action today! We are to guard ourselves against deception by staying in the Word so that we will have a clear understanding of right and wrong. We are to trust the Holy Spirit for discernment, truth, guidance, wise counsel, and peace; it is the Holy Spirit who establishes order and unity of spirit. We are to endure, being steadfast in our faith and persistent in our good works. And we are to do our utmost to get the gospel to all the world as a witness to all nations.

We have our marching orders! The signs of the times around us may be terrifying, but if we remain focused on the things we are to be doing to prepare for Christ's return, we will be obedient to the Lord's commands and will know His salvation. We may not know the precise time of the Lord's coming, but we *do* know from God's Word what we are to be doing with our time. We know what we are to be doing as the signs of His coming unfold around us.

> If you abide in My word, you are My disciples indeed. And you shall know the truth, and the truth shall make you free.
>
> —John 8:31–32

❧ What does it mean to abide in Jesus' word? How is this done?

47

❧ Why is abiding in the word so important in understanding God's plan for the future?

❧ Today and Tomorrow ❧

TODAY: GOD HAS GIVEN ME CLEAR INSTRUCTIONS ON HOW TO LIVE IN THESE DAYS.

TOMORROW: I WILL GUARD AGAINST DECEPTION AND SHARE THE GOSPEL WITH OTHERS.

An Imminent Surprise

ᡠ In This Lesson ᡐ

LEARNING: IF I KNOW THAT JESUS IS COMING AGAIN, HOW CAN IT BE A SURPRISE?

GROWING: WHAT ATTITUDE SHOULD WE HAVE TOWARD CHRIST'S RETURN?

The coming of the Lord is going to be a surprise—a welcome, joyous, glorious surprise—to the world at large and to those who are believers in Christ Jesus. The Christian's approach to this surprise is very different, however, from that of nonbelievers. We who have accepted Jesus as our Savior should expect this surprise, even to the extent of feeling a great urgency, because we believe that the surprise is imminent, close at hand.

A Joyous Surprise

Jesus made a number of statements about the surprise element of His return. He said:

Then two men will be in the field: one will be taken and the other left. Two women will be grinding at the mill: one will be taken and the other left. Watch therefore, for you do not know what hour your Lord is coming. But know this, that if the master of the house had known what hour the thief would come, he would have watched and not allowed his house to be broken into. Therefore you also be ready, for the Son of Man is coming at an hour when you do not expect.

—Matthew 24:40–44

∽ Why did Jesus use everyday working situations to illustrate the day of His return? What does this indicate about that day?

∽ Why did Jesus also use the metaphor of a thief stealing from a house? How does this apply to His return to earth?

Earlier in this same chapter of Matthew, Jesus said that life would be "as the days of Noah" at His return. People would be eating, drinking, and getting married—life as usual, all things seemingly normal. His coming would be a great surprise, just as it was to those who were not aware of what was happening until Noah entered the ark and the floodwaters began to rise.

The coming of the Lord will be without a sounded alarm, without warning sirens, without an opportunity to utter the words "I believe in Christ Jesus." It will be swift and immediate.

A Constant State of Readiness

The Lord's return is an imminent surprise, so we are commanded to be ready. Indeed, we are to live in a constant state of readiness for that moment. Jesus said:

Take heed, watch and pray; for you do not know when the time is. It is like a man going to a far country, who left his house and gave authority to his servants, and to each his work, and commanded the doorkeeper to watch. Watch therefore, for you do not know when the master of the house is coming—in the evening, at midnight, at the crowing of the rooster, or in the morning—lest, coming suddenly, he find you sleeping. And what I say to you, I say to all: Watch!

—Mark 13:33–37

‌✍ Note that, in these verses, Jesus switched His metaphor from a thief robbing a house to being Himself the Master of the house. What does this teach about His return?

‌✍ What does it mean to be found sleeping? In what ways do Christians "sleep" concerning the Lord's coming? What will result for those who are found asleep?

Watch and pray. Note in the preceding passage that the Lord tells His disciples to watch and pray. We are to be petitioning God as we await the Lord's coming. On the night of His betrayal as Jesus prayed in the Garden of Gethsemane, He said to His disciple Simon, "I have prayed for you, that your faith should not fail" (Luke 22:32). Surely we need to have this same prayer for ourselves: that our faith will not fail.

We must pray that we will not give in to temptation. Jesus said to His disciples, "Pray that you may not enter into temptation" (Luke 22:40). We must pray that we will not be deceived. Jesus warned, "False christs and false prophets will rise and show signs and wonders to deceive, if possible, even the elect" (Mark 13:22). We must pray for discernment and an absolute understanding of right and wrong.

We must pray that those of us who are in Christ will continue to love one another and to fulfill Christ's commandments. As you read through the final prayer of Jesus for His disciples, make this prayer your own. Personalize it for yourself and your family:

"Father, the hour has come. Glorify Your Son, that Your Son also may glorify You, as You have given Him authority over all flesh, that He should give eternal life to as many as You have given Him. And this is eternal life, that they may know You, the only true God, and Jesus Christ whom You have sent. I have glorified You on the earth. I have finished the work which You have given Me to do. And now, O Father, glorify Me together with Yourself, with the glory which I had with You before the world was.

"I have manifested Your name to the men whom You have given Me out of the world. They were Yours, You gave them to Me, and they have kept Your word. Now they have known that all things which You have given Me are from You. For I have given to them the words which You have given Me; and they have received them, and have known surely that I came forth from You; and they have believed that You sent Me.

"I pray for them. I do not pray for the world but for those whom You have given Me, for they are Yours. And all Mine are Yours, and Yours are Mine, and I am glorified in them. Now I am no longer in the world, but these are in the world, and I come to You. Holy Father, keep through Your name those whom You have given Me, that they may be one as We are. While I was with them in the world, I kept them in Your name. Those whom You gave Me I have kept; and none of them is lost except the son of perdition, that the Scripture might be fulfilled. But now I come to You, and these things I speak in the world, that they may have My joy fulfilled in themselves. I have given them Your word; and the world has hated them because they are not of the world, just as I am not of the world. I do not pray that You should take them out of the world, but that You should keep them from the evil one. They are not of the world, just as I am not of the world. Sanctify them by Your truth. Your word is truth. As You sent Me into the world, I also have sent them into the world. And for their sakes I sanctify Myself, that they also may be sanctified by the truth.

"I do not pray for these alone, but also for those who will believe in Me through their word; that they all may be one, as You, Father, are in Me, and I in You; that they also may be one in Us, that the world may believe that You sent Me. And the glory which You gave Me I have given them, that they may be one just as We are one: I in them, and You in Me; that they may be made perfect in one, and that the world may know that You have sent Me, and have loved them as You have loved Me."

—John 17:1–23

54

🕭 List below the specific things Jesus prayed for His disciples in this passage. What does each request mean, in practical terms?

An active, expectant watch. To watch means to be actively looking. It is expectant watching. Jesus gave a number of signs that would precede His coming and then He spoke this parable to His disciples:

> Look at the fig tree, and all the trees. When they are already budding, you see and know for yourselves that summer is now near. So you also, when you see these things happening, know that the kingdom of God is near. Assuredly, I say to you, this generation will by no means pass away till all things take place. Heaven and earth will pass away, but My words will by no means pass away.
>
> —Luke 21:29–33

I want you to note three things in this brief passage. First, Jesus knew what all men in Israel knew at that time: a budding tree was a sign of spring. Fruit was going to be produced; a harvest was coming. We are to be looking for signs of harvest. Now for a harvest to be produced, a seed must first be planted and cultivated. A tree must be pruned, trained up, watered, and nurtured if it is to be a healthy tree that produces fruit. As we await the coming of the Lord, we are to be about "fruit production." We are to be planting seeds of the gospel in fertile soil, nurturing the spiritual growth of others, and bearing the fruit of the Spirit in anticipation of Christ's return. We are to be looking for fruit, expecting revival, and working toward it.

Second, Jesus said that the people who saw these preliminary signs of His coming would know that the kingdom of God was coming within a generation. A generation is several decades; in Scripture it is usually a period of forty years. Again, we have confirmation that we will not know the day, hour, week, month, year, or even decade of Christ's return. But we are to have a growing sense of urgency that His coming is close—it is within a generation.

There is a major difference in how we live and what we choose to do with our time if we believe that something is going to happen within our lifetime and may even happen at any moment. We live with a much greater concern about how we spend our time and our resources. We do our work, but always with one eye open to the Lord's appearing. We enjoy our lives, but always in anticipation that the Lord may appear at any moment.

There is nothing in the Scriptures that would preclude the Lord Jesus coming in this generation. Are we alert to that possibility? Are we eagerly anticipating that today may be the day?

Third, Jesus spoke these great words of comfort: "Heaven and earth will pass away, but My words will by no means pass away" (v. 33). All that Jesus has said about His coming *will* occur. We can count on Jesus' words to be true.

> But the end of all things is at hand; therefore be serious and watchful in your prayers. And above all things have fervent love for one another, for *"love will cover a multitude of sins."*
>
> —1 Peter 4:7–8

What does it mean to be serious in your prayers? To be watchful?

In practical terms, what is "fervent love"? What other types of love are there?

❧ Why are Christians commanded to love one another in preparation for Christ's return?

❧ Today and Tomorrow ❧

TODAY: JESUS COMMANDED ME TO WATCH AND PRAY FOR HIS RETURN.

TOMORROW: I WILL PRAY DAILY THIS WEEK FOR THE LORD TO PREPARE ME FOR HIS KINGDOM.

Three Parables About the Lord's Return

─── ❧ **In This Lesson** ☙ ───

LEARNING: WHAT IS GOD'S KINGDOM LIKE?

GROWING: WHAT PART DO I PLAY IN THAT KINGDOM?

❧

The bulk of Jesus' teaching about His return can be found in Matthew 24–25, Mark 13, and Luke 21. I encourage you to read these four chapters in their entirety. In Matthew 25 we find two well-known parables that are directly related to the end of the age and Christ's return. They deal directly with our preparation for Christ's return.

The Parable of the Ten Virgins

As you read through the following parable, take special note of the fact that nobody knew the precise timing of the bridegroom's arrival for his bride. This was customary in Jesus' day. A man and wife were betrothed, legally bound to each other in a ceremony between the two families (at which the bride might not even be in attendance), but the bride and groom did not live together or have a sexual relationship until the time of their wedding. The wedding might take place as long as a year after the betrothal.

During this period between betrothal and wedding, the bridegroom prepared a home for his bride and set things in order for their life together. The bride prepared herself physically and emotionally for her marriage. The bridegroom might come at any time for his bride, and her responsibility was to be ready to go at a moment's notice.

After the bridegroom claimed his bride from her father's house, he escorted her back to their new home, with those in the wedding party lighting the way, singing and dancing joyously in a grand procession through the streets of the village. A wedding feast was held, generally lasting a full week, at which time the bride and groom were crowned the king and queen of their new home and many blessings were voiced. A wedding was one of the most wonderful celebrations in the life of any person in Bible times.

Jesus said to His disciples that He was going to prepare a place for them and that He would return for them (John 14:2–3). He is clearly the bridegroom in this parable. The bride is the church for whom the bridegroom is coming. The virgins are the attendants of the bride, the ones who accompany the bride and expect to be part of the wedding party for the entire celebration. Jesus said:

> "Then the kingdom of heaven shall be likened to ten virgins who took their lamps and went out to meet the bridegroom. Now five of them were wise, and five were foolish. Those who were foolish took their lamps and took no oil with them, but the wise took oil in their vessels with their lamps. But while the bridegroom was delayed, they all slumbered and slept.
>
> "And at midnight a cry was heard: 'Behold, the bridegroom is coming; go out to meet him!' Then all those virgins arose and trimmed their lamps. And the foolish said to the wise, 'Give us some of your oil, for our lamps are going out.' But the wise an-

swered, saying, 'No, lest there should not be enough for us and you; but go rather to those who sell, and buy for yourselves.' And while they went to buy, the bridegroom came, and those who were ready went in with him to the wedding; and the door was shut.

"Afterward the other virgins came also, saying, 'Lord, Lord, open to us!' But he answered and said, 'Assuredly, I say to you, I do not know you.'

"Watch therefore, for you know neither the day nor the hour in which the Son of Man is coming."

—Matthew 25:1–13

What do the lamps and oil represent in this parable? What does it mean to have a lamp but no oil?

Why were the foolish virgins shut out from the wedding feast? What does this teach about having no "oil" for one's "lamp"?

⤜ Notice that both the wise and the foolish in this parable fell asleep. How does this compare with Lesson 5, where we were commanded to be watchful?

I want you to note four things in this parable that relate to our preparation for Christ's return. First, those in the wedding party "slumbered and slept" because the bridegroom was delayed. There are many in the church today who have stopped looking for the Lord's return; some don't even believe that He is coming again. They are asleep or drowsy when it comes to Christ's coming.

Second, the virgins who did not have sufficient oil in their lamps had plenty of time to purchase oil, trim the wicks of their lamps, and get ready for the bridegroom's coming. They were not unprepared because of a lack of knowledge or a lack of time. They were unprepared because they simply did not do what they should have.

Third, the wise virgins did not share their oil because they could not share. None of us can give the Holy Spirit to another person.

Fourth, the lack of preparation on the part of the five foolish virgins resulted in their being shut out of the wedding feast. They missed the joy of the processional, and they missed the celebration. The consequence of their lack of preparation is great.

What does it mean to have sufficient oil in our lamps? Oil throughout the Scriptures is a symbol of the Holy Spirit. The Holy Spirit comes to dwell within us when we receive Jesus as our Savior, but it is up to us daily to ask the Holy Spirit to fill us. This daily filling of the Holy Spirit means that we submit ourselves to Him and seek His guidance, direction, and counsel for all that we say and do. We submit our will to His will, saying as Jesus said, "not My will, but Yours, be done." We are willing to follow the leading of the Holy Spirit as we face each decision, confront each problem, or encounter each person who comes across our path.

The Holy Spirit operates in us according to the degree that we invite Him to do so. It is up to us, as an act of our will, to ask that He fill us daily. Those who do not have oil in their lamps are those who attend church but have never confessed their sin to the Lord, believed in the atoning sacrifice of Jesus Christ on the cross, or received God's forgiveness of their sin and the presence of His Spirit. They have played at church but have not been genuinely saved.

This parable stands also as a great warning to those who are lukewarm in their commitment to the Lord, and those who are not actively following the Lord.

The Parable of the Three Servants

Jesus also taught this parable about His return:

> "For the kingdom of heaven is like a man traveling to a far country, who called his own servants and delivered his goods to them. And to one he gave five talents, to another two, and to another one, to each according to his own ability; and immediately he went on a journey. Then he who had received the five

talents went and traded with them, and made another five talents. And likewise he who had received two gained two more also. But he who had received one went and dug in the ground, and hid his lord's money. After a long time the lord of those servants came and settled accounts with them.

"So he who had received five talents came and brought five other talents, saying, 'Lord, you delivered to me five talents; look, I have gained five more talents besides them.' His lord said to him, 'Well done, good and faithful servant; you were faithful over a few things, I will make you ruler over many things. Enter into the joy of your lord.' He also who had received two talents came and said, 'Lord, you delivered to me two talents; look, I have gained two more talents besides them.' His lord said to him, 'Well done, good and faithful servant; you have been faithful over a few things, I will make you ruler over many things. Enter into the joy of your lord.'

"Then he who had received the one talent came and said, 'Lord, I knew you to be a hard man, reaping where you have not sown, and gathering where you have not scattered seed. And I was afraid, and went and hid your talent in the ground. Look, there you have what is yours.'

"But his lord answered and said to him, 'You wicked and lazy servant, you knew that I reap where I have not sown, and gather where I have not scattered seed. So you ought to have deposited my money with the bankers, and at my coming I would have received back my own with interest. So take the talent from him, and give it to him who has ten talents.

'For to everyone who has, more will be given, and he will have abundance; but from him who does not have, even what he has will be taken away. And cast the unprofitable servant into the outer darkness. There will be weeping and gnashing of teeth.'"

—Matthew 25:14–30

What does this parable teach about the kingdom of God? How does a person make a profit in spiritual terms?

In spiritual terms, what sort of person was the man who buried his master's money? What is the spiritual equivalent of his attitude?

I would like to call your attention to three specific things in this parable. First, this parable is about the kingdom of heaven. It is a spiritual story about a spiritual kingdom. We may see principles related to the wise use of our material resources and even the wise use of our God-given talents and aptitudes that we have from birth, but this story is primarily about spiritual matters.

Second, the one thing that the Lord Jesus gave to those who followed Him as He prepared to go to the Father in heaven was the Holy Spirit. He said, "I will pray the Father, and He will give you another Helper, that He may abide with you forever—the Spirit of truth, whom the world cannot receive, because it neither sees Him nor knows Him; but you know Him, for He dwells with you and will be in you. I will not leave you orphans; I will come to you" (John 14:16–18). Part of the Holy Spirit's function in our lives is to remind us of the words of Jesus and the commandments of Jesus (John 15:26–27).

When we receive the Holy Spirit into our lives, we automatically receive two things that He imparts: one or more spiritual gifts (Rom. 12:4–8) and the fruit-bearing nature of the Holy Spirit, which we manifest in our lives the more we abide in the Lord and in His Word (John 15:5–8; Gal. 5:22–23). If we apply these principles to the parable of the three servants, we see that these servants have been given *spiritual* talents. It is the Lord's intent that we use them. And as we do, He does a multiplying work in us and through us to others. He takes the use of our spiritual gifts and the fruit of our character to build up the wealth of souls and strong believers in His kingdom.

Third, the servant who did not use his spiritual gift, even in the easiest way, was severely reprimanded. In sharp contrast, both of the servants who invested their talents experienced a doubling of their talents and were rewarded with more spiritual gifts and great joy! The question that each of us must ask is this: What am I doing with the spiritual gifts imparted to me by the Holy Spirit?

Having then gifts differing according to the grace that is given to us, let us use them: if prophecy, let us prophesy in proportion to our faith; or ministry, let us use it in our ministering; he who teaches, in teaching; he who exhorts, in exhortation; he who gives, with liberality; he who leads, with diligence; he who shows mercy, with cheerfulness.

—Romans 12:6–8

🔊 Give practical examples of each of the following gifts:

Prophecy:

Ministry:

Teaching:

Exhortation:

Giving:

Mercy:

67

The Parable of the Working and Watching Servants

In Mark 13 we have a third parable the Lord taught about His return:

> Take heed, watch and pray; for you do not know when the time is. It is like a man going to a far country, who left his house and gave authority to his servants, and to each his work, and commanded the doorkeeper to watch. Watch therefore, for you do not know when the master of the house is coming—in the evening, at midnight, at the crowing of the rooster, or in the morning—lest, coming suddenly, he find you sleeping.
>
> —Mark 13:33–36

Notice that this man gave authority and work to each of his servants before he went to a far country. Jesus also gave His disciples authority over all manifestations of evil (Mark 16:17–18) and gave them work assignments, specifically the work of being witnesses, winning souls, and preaching and teaching the gospel in all nations (Matt. 28:18–20).

Also like the master in this parable, Jesus gave an additional command. As His servants, we are to do our work with His authority, and we are to watch for His return (Mark 13:37). We are to live in anticipation of His coming.

> Then He said to them, "The harvest truly is great, but the laborers are few; therefore pray the Lord of the harvest to send out laborers into His harvest."
>
> —Luke 10:2

What harvest was Jesus referring to here? Who are the laborers? What labor will they perform?

Why are there few laborers? Why did Jesus command His disciples to pray for more laborers? How might God use you to answer that prayer?

Today and Tomorrow

TODAY: THE LORD HAS COMMANDED ME TO BE AN ACTIVE PART IN HIS KINGDOM.

TOMORROW: I WILL ASK THE LORD TO USE ME THIS WEEK TO SHARE THE GOSPEL WITH OTHERS.

∽ **Notes and Prayer Requests:** ∽

Lesson 7

Why Is Jesus Coming Again?

---------------- ᥐ **In This Lesson** ᥐ ----------------

Learning: What is God's reason for sending Jesus to earth twice?

Growing: What does His plan have to do with me?

⌇

Perhaps the central question to the Lord's return is one that very few people ever stop to consider: Why is Jesus coming again? The short and simple answer is this: to finish the work that He began the first time He walked the earth. The question then needs to be asked, why did Jesus come the first time? If we know why Jesus came the first time, we have our answer to why He is coming again. His first coming is our backdrop for understanding what He will finish when He comes again.

The Scriptures give us five distinct reasons why Jesus came to the earth as a baby born in Bethlehem, to live and die, to be raised from the dead, and to ascend back to heaven. Those reasons, in summary, are:

1. To fulfill the law.

2. To reveal the Father.

3. To testify to the truth.

4. To seek and save the lost.

5. To reveal life at its best.

In this lesson we will take a brief look at each of these reasons and the way these purposes of Christ are going to be fulfilled when He comes again. We also see in these five purposes the distinct ways in which we are to prepare ourselves for His coming.

To Fulfill the Law

Jesus said of Himself, "Do not think that I came to destroy the Law or the Prophets. I did not come to destroy but to fulfill. For assuredly, I say to you, till heaven and earth pass away, one jot or one tittle will by no means pass from the law till all is fulfilled" (Matt. 5:17–18). Jesus came to fulfill a two-part law—first, the moral law as given to Moses, primarily the Ten Commandments. These laws regarding human behavior in relationship to God and man are God's unchanging standard for regulating the conduct of mankind. This moral law applies to all people, Gentiles and Jews alike. It is in effect even for nonbelievers, even though they may not acknowledge it and may routinely break it.

The second aspect of law that Jesus came to fulfill was the legislative, judicial, and ceremonial system that was handed down to Moses. This law pertains only to the Jews and does not apply to Gentiles.

Obviously, from what Jesus said in Matthew 5:17, to fulfill the law is not to replace it or put an end to it. Jesus lived in obedience to the law. He fulfilled it in these ways: He lived out all of the signs and predictions made in the Old Testament about the Messiah, and He died as the final, definitive, atoning sacrifice for sin. In addition, He came to explain the full meaning of the moral law. In the Sermon on the Mount

(Matt. 5–7), we see a number of instances in which Jesus went beyond the letter of the law to explain fully the spirit of the law and the meaning undergirding it.

Jesus said that He came to fulfill the law and the prophets. In Matthew 22:37–40, Jesus said, "'You shall love the LORD your God with all your heart, with all your soul, and with all your mind.' This is the first and great commandment. And the second is like it: 'You shall love your neighbor as yourself.' On these two commandments hang all the Law and the Prophets." Jesus came to fulfill the words of the prophets, who repeatedly called the people to obedience to God's commandments and admonished them in the way they were to live. Jesus fulfilled the prophets by showing us how to love God with our whole heart, soul, and mind, and how to love our neighbors as ourselves.

🕭 What does it mean that Jesus came to "fulfill the law"? In what ways did He do this?

🕭 Why did Jesus not abolish the law? What does this teach about the Old Testament's principles, such as the Ten Commandments?

Jesus was the Father's full expression of how a human being is to live. Jesus embodied all of the law in the way that He lived His life, and in so doing He showed us that it is possible to keep the letter of the law only if we first choose to keep the spirit of the law.

When Christ comes again, He calls those who have believed in Him to the ultimate expression of a law fulfilled. His law will become the law of the entire world. We will live forever in a state of worship before the Father, serving Him and praising Him with all of our heart, soul, and mind. And we will live in a state of complete harmony and unity with all other believers. Our challenge as we prepare for the Lord's return is to be worshiping God in the fullness of our own lives. We are to be expressing love to others at all times.

> I say then: Walk in the Spirit, and you shall not fulfill the lust of the flesh. For the flesh lusts against the Spirit, and the Spirit against the flesh; and these are contrary to one another, so that you do not do the things that you wish. But if you are led by the Spirit, you are not under the law.
>
> —Galatians 5:16–18

If Jesus came to fulfill the law, why does Paul say that we are not under the law? What does being "led by the Spirit" have to do with this equation?

🙞 Notice that Paul speaks of fulfilling the lust of the flesh and Jesus spoke of fulfilling the law. How is lust like a law of the flesh?

To Reveal the Father

Jesus prayed to His Father, "You loved Me before the foundation of the world. O righteous Father! The world has not known You, but I have known You; and these have known that You sent Me. And I have declared to them Your name, and will declare it, that the love with which You loved Me may be in them" (John 17:24–26). Jesus came to show us the nature of God, and specifically the nature of God as our heavenly Father.

Throughout the generations God had revealed Himself in a progressive revelation to His people. He gave them various names by which they might know Him. In revealing Himself as *Elohim*, He revealed His infinite power and faithfulness. In revealing His name *Yahweh*, He revealed that He was the eternal One, in personal relationship with His people. He gave His name *Adonai* to show that He was the Master and Lord of His people.

When Jesus came, He summed up all the names of God previously revealed in one word: *Father*. It is from our loving heavenly Father that all things come. We are to relate to the Father as children relate to a loving, generous, just, and always-present daddy. We are to know that, just as a child bears the likeness of his father, so we are to bear the likeness of God our Father in the way we live and treat others.

A person cannot fully know God apart from Jesus. There is no other means for discovering the forgiveness of God, the fact that God answers prayer, the way in which God meets needs, or the personal meaning of life. There is no other basis on which to have hope for resurrection and life after death.

When Jesus comes again, He will fulfill His role as *Messiah*, which has also been translated "Delivering Prince." Jesus is the Prince and our Father is the sovereign King. When Jesus returns, we will have a full understanding that He is King of kings and Lord of lords. He is the full reflection of the sovereign One, bearing all of the authority and power of a king. Furthermore, we who believe in Him will rule and reign with Him.

We are to prepare for the coming of our "daddy" King by preparing ourselves as His children, His princes. We are to become like Christ in every way, doing all we can to grow into the fullness of Christ's character.

For it pleased the Father that in Him all the fullness should dwell, and by Him to reconcile all things to Himself, by Him, whether things on earth or things in heaven, having made peace through the blood of His cross.

—Colossians 1:19–20

What does it mean that "all the fullness" of God dwells in Jesus?

What does it mean that Jesus reconciled all things to Himself?

To Testify to the Truth

Pilate asked Jesus, "Are You a king then?" Jesus answered, "You say rightly that I am a king. For this cause I was born, and for this cause I have come into the world, that I should bear witness to the truth. Everyone who is of the truth hears My voice" (John 18:37). Perhaps the most succinct statement of His truth is found in John 3:

> "Most assuredly, I say to you, unless one is born of water and the Spirit, he cannot enter the kingdom of God. That which is born of the flesh is flesh, and that which is born of the Spirit is spirit. Do not marvel that I said to you, 'You must be born again.' The wind blows where it wishes, and you hear the sound of it, but cannot tell where it comes from and where it goes. So is everyone who is born of the Spirit....

> "No one has ascended to heaven but He who came down from heaven, that is, the Son of Man who is in heaven.... For God so loved the world that He gave His only begotten Son, that whoever believes in Him should not perish but have everlasting life. For God did not send His Son into the world to condemn the world, but that the world through Him might be saved.

> "He who believes in Him is not condemned; but he who does not believe is condemned already, because he has not believed in the name of the only begotten Son of God.... Everyone practicing evil hates the light and does not come to the light, lest his deeds should be exposed. But he who does the truth comes to the light, that his deeds may be clearly seen, that they have been done in God."

> —John 3:5–8, 13, 16–18, 20–21

What does it mean to be "born of water and the Spirit"? Have you been born again in that way?

What did Jesus mean when He compared the Spirit to the wind? What does this reveal about His second coming?

The truth that Jesus came to proclaim can perhaps be summed up in one sentence: God desires that man be set free from the bondage of sin and guilt and be fully reconciled in love to God and to one another. Jesus is the full embodiment of that truth (John 14:6).

When Jesus comes again, He comes to set us free from all temptation to sin. When we are with Him, we will be totally beyond the bounds of evil influence; we will be freed from a world that still groans under the weight of sin. We will be in the loving presence of God the Father without any inhibiting influence of our fleshly nature.

In preparing for the Lord's return, we are to seek God's righteousness in all we say, do, think, and believe. We are to pursue the truth at all times and become quick to discern deceit and lies in all their many forms.

> Jesus said to him, "I am the way, the truth, and the life. No one comes to the Father except through Me."

> —John 14:6

Define how Jesus is each of the following:

The way:

The truth:

The life:

➷ How does this teaching conflict with the world's teachings?

To Seek and Save the Lost

Jesus said, "The Son of Man has come to seek and to save that which was lost" (Luke 19:10). In Jesus' great parable of the loving father (also called the parable of the prodigal son), Jesus paints this picture of God the Father: "When he [the prodigal son] was still a great way off, his father saw him and had compassion, and ran and fell on his neck and kissed him" (Luke 15:20). What a wonderful picture this is of our loving heavenly Father! He is forever seeking our return to Him. He is continually seeking our salvation from our old selves.

The result of seeking is finding. Jesus said, "Seek, and you will find" (Matt. 7:7). When Jesus comes again, we will be fully found and saved from all sin forever. We, in turn, will fully find our Lord; we will know Him in dimensions we cannot even imagine now. We will also know ourselves and others as God knows us (1 Cor. 13:12).

As we await the Lord's return, we must continually seek to know the Lord more intimately. We must understand ourselves so that we can release old wounds to the Lord and be healed of them. We must desire spiritual growth, continually working out our salvation in practical ways so that we might become increasingly whole as human beings in spirit, mind, and body.

> When I was a child, I spoke as a child, I understood as a child, I thought as a child; but when I became a man, I put away childish things. For now we see in a mirror, dimly, but then face to face. Now I know in part, but then I shall know just as I also am known.
>
> —1 Corinthians 13:11–12

In what ways is it childish to have an imperfect understanding of God's character? Give examples of childish beliefs and of mature beliefs.

🖛 Why does Paul say that we view God as though looking in a mirror? How is seeing someone face-to-face different from seeing that person's reflection?

To Reveal Life at Its Best

Jesus said, "I have come that they may have life, and that they may have it more abundantly" (John 10:10). Jesus came to reveal two things by the example of His own life: the fact that we can have an abundant life and the way to live an abundant life.

A life in Christ is marked by what we call the fruit of the Holy Spirit: love, joy, and peace. It is a life marked by freedom from guilt and sin, a life of reconciliation to others as manifested in forgiveness, patience, goodness, faithfulness, and gentleness. It is a life marked by self-control and victory over the lust of the flesh, the lust of the eyes, and the pride of life. It is the life that every person longs to live (Gal. 5:22–23).

When Jesus comes again, He will add the crowning facet to the abundant life: perfection for all eternity. He will take abundance to the highest degree, bringing us to a fullness of love, joy, and peace. He will provide that perfection to the greatest degree of time and space, to all eternity.

We are to prepare for His coming by walking in the Spirit and bearing more and more fruit of the Spirit in our lives. To walk in the Spirit is to know the abundant life of Christ and to know a life beyond compare.

Now to Him who is able to do exceedingly abundantly above all that we ask or think, according to the power that works in us, to Him be glory in the church by Christ Jesus to all generations, forever and ever.

—Ephesians 3:20–21

 Notice the adjectives Paul uses to describe God's provisions: "exceedingly," "abundantly," "above all." What do these teach about His character?

⇜ When has God gone far beyond your wildest expectations in your life? What does this suggest about His kingdom in eternity?

⇜ Today and Tomorrow ⇝

TODAY: JESUS IS COMING AGAIN IN ORDER TO FULLY REVEAL THE FATHER TO THE WORLD.

TOMORROW: I WILL SPEND TIME THIS WEEK LEARNING MORE ABOUT THE CHARACTER OF GOD AS REVEALED IN THE BIBLE.

∽∞∾ Notes and Prayer Requests: ∽∞∾

LESSON 8

The Rapture of the Church

───── ❧ **In This Lesson** ❧ ─────

LEARNING: WHAT IS THE RAPTURE?

GROWING: WHAT WILL CHRISTIANS EXPERIENCE WHEN THAT DAY COMES?

❧

One of the great hopes and joys of those who may be alive when the Lord returns is a biblical event called the Rapture, also called the snatching away or taking away of the church. As we mentioned earlier in this book, the word *Rapture* is not in the Bible, but we read about it in 1 Thessalonians 4:15–18:

> For this we say to you by the word of the Lord, that we who are alive and remain until the coming of the Lord will by no means precede those who are asleep. For the Lord Himself will descend from heaven with a shout, with the voice of an archangel, and with the trumpet of God. And the dead in Christ will rise first. Then we who are alive and remain shall be caught up together with them in the clouds to meet the Lord in the air. And thus we shall always be with the Lord. Therefore comfort one another with these words.

I want to call your attention to four aspects of this passage in Thessalonians. First, the Lord is the One who is calling His people. Those who are unsaved are not able to hear His voice (John 10:4–5). The Rapture is only for believers.

Second, the Lord calls from heaven and we respond instantly to His call. In Revelation 4:1 we read, "After these things I looked, and behold, a door standing open in heaven. And the first voice which I heard was like a trumpet speaking with me." The Lord's voice is a heralding, trumpet-like call to us, a signal to which we hearken and respond. In the Greek language in which this passage was first written, the word *shout* refers to a military officer barking a command. The trumpet is used to herald the assembling of a group of people. When we hear the Lord calling to us, we will have no hesitation in our obedience.

Third, the Lord's call will be a summons to all believers, both those alive at that time and those who have died. A woman once told me about a summer camp experience she had: "They had a bell that they would ring. It was a signal that we were all to gather together immediately in the central courtyard. It didn't matter if you were in a cabin or in the dining hall or playing softball or swimming in the pool. When the bell rang, you quit what you were doing and immediately went to the courtyard. There were some parents at the camp who had been campers when they were children—and when the bell sounded, even these parents left what they were doing and went to the courtyard." That's the way the Lord's summons will be for us. The dead who are with the Lord and about His business in heaven will come immediately. We who are alive and on earth will come immediately. We will all be gathered together as one body.

Fourth, we will never be separated from the Lord again. The Rapture is not a brief, rapturous experience in which we feel caught up in the Holy Spirit. It is a permanent shifting of our existence. We will be forever with the Lord from that moment on.

Why will the Rapture include Christians who are alive as well as those who have died previously? What does this suggest about God's eternal purposes?

Why is the Rapture only for Christians? What will happen to those who have rejected Christ?

An Immediate Change

The Rapture will elicit an immediate response from us and result in an immediate change in us. Paul wrote to the Corinthians:

> We shall not all sleep, but we shall all be changed—in a moment, in the twinkling of an eye, at the last trumpet. For the trumpet will sound, and the dead will be raised incorruptible, and we shall be changed. For this corruptible must put on incorruption, and this mortal must put on immortality. So when this corruptible has put on incorruption, and this mortal has put on immortality, then shall be brought to pass the saying that is written: "Death is swallowed up in victory."
>
> —1 Corinthians 15:51–54

How did Jesus' death and resurrection swallow up death? What does this mean for those who reject His salvation?

 Notice that Paul refers to this event as "the last trumpet". What other "trumpets" has the Lord used in the past? Why is this the last one?

In Bible times the twinkling in a person's eye was considered to be the briefest unit of time possible. Quickly here, quickly gone. That is the nature of the Rapture. In a moment so brief and instantaneous that we cannot measure it, we will be raised and changed. In that moment we will receive glorified bodies. The bodies we currently know as our flesh will be instantly changed into physical form that is recognizable but does not decay or experience sickness, pain, or limitation. It is because our bodies are changed instantly that we are able to respond instantly to the Lord's call.

The Rapture also results in our physical removal from earth. Jesus said, "Two men will be in the field: one will be taken and the other left. Two women will be grinding at the mill: one will be taken and the other left" (Matt. 24:40–41). We will be changed in the Rapture, and the nature of the whole earth will also be changed. Those who are indwelt by the Holy Spirit will be removed from the earth.

A Judgment for Christians

The change we experience in the moment of the Rapture will include an instant judgment of those who are believers. We cannot enter the presence of the Lord and remain there forever without this judgment. The judgment Christians face is not related to sin but to our works as believers. To be in the presence of the Lord is to see instantly the full scope of our works as the Lord sees them.

Read how John describes the appearance of the Lord: "I heard behind me a loud voice, as of a trumpet.... Then I turned to see the voice that spoke with me. And having turned I saw seven golden lampstands, and in the midst of the seven lampstands One like the Son of Man, clothed with a garment down to the feet and girded about the chest with a golden band. His head and His hair were white like wool, as white as snow, and His eyes like a flame of fire" (Rev. 1:10, 12–14).

When the Lord looks at us with His eyes of fire, we will be known fully by Him and we will fully know ourselves. We will see all that we didn't do, all that we could have done and could have been. All that wasn't and isn't will be burned up by His holiness, and what remains will be of Him. It will be eternal, it will be pure, and it will be rewarded. The more that remains, the greater the reward. Paul also wrote of this to the Corinthians:

> According to the grace of God which was given to me, as a wise master builder I have laid the foundation, and another builds on it. But let each one take heed how he builds on it. For no other foundation can anyone lay than that which is laid, which is Jesus Christ. Now if anyone builds on this foundation with gold, silver, precious stones, wood, hay, straw, each one's work will become clear; for the Day will declare it, because it will be

92

revealed by fire; and the fire will test each one's work, of what sort it is. If anyone's work which he has built on it endures, he will receive a reward. If anyone's work is burned, he will suffer loss; but he himself will be saved, yet so as through fire.

—1 Corinthians 3:10–15

❧ What is Paul referring to when he speaks of us building on Jesus' foundation? In what ways do Christians build within God's kingdom?

❧ What types of buildings are made of gold and silver? What deeds are of hay and straw? How can you tell the difference between them?

The purpose of God's judgment of our works is to burn away anything that is not of the Lord so that we might be completely pure as we enter into His eternal presence. This final refinement of our souls produces in us the glory of the Lord as we enter into a state in which we are never separated from the Lord. It creates holiness and wholeness in us so that we are completely without fault, sin, or any desire to sin. What a great and glorious day that will be for us!

> But who can endure the day of His coming? And who can stand when He appears? For He is like a refiner's fire and like launderers' soap. He will sit as a refiner and a purifier of silver; He will purify the sons of Levi, and purge them as gold and silver, that they may offer to the LORD an offering in righteousness.
>
> —Malachi 3:2–3

❧ Notice the analogies used here for God's purification: fire, caustic soap, etc. What do these suggest about God's character? About His purifying process?

How does this apply to the Rapture? How is it different from God's eternal judgment on sin?

Beware of Mockers

Peter warned that the Rapture is such a mysterious and awesome event that there will be those who scoff at the very idea, saying it isn't rational or scientific. He wrote:

> Beloved, I now write to you ... that you may be mindful of the words which were spoken before by the holy prophets, and of the commandment of us, the apostles of the Lord and Savior, knowing this first: that scoffers will come in the last days, walking according to their own lusts, and saying, "Where is the promise of His coming? For since the fathers fell asleep, all things continue as they were from the beginning of creation."
>
> —2 Peter 3:1–4

✍ Have you ever encountered someone who scoffs at the idea of the Rapture? Have you ever doubted it yourself?

✍ On what basis can we be certain that Jesus will return to earth? Why should you believe the Bible rather than the world's teachings?

The Lord is going to call for His people. He will bring us into His presence, a purified people to live with Him forever. And the Rapture will be instantaneous. There will be no opportunity for any response to the Rapture other than to participate in it fully if one is a believer in Christ Jesus, or to be left out of it completely if one is not. It may seem as though His appearance has been delayed, but all things are in God's perfect timing. As Peter wrote:

> But, beloved, do not forget this one thing, that with the Lord one day is as a thousand years, and a thousand years as one day. The Lord is not slack concerning His promise, as some count slackness, but is longsuffering toward us, not willing that any should perish but that all should come to repentance.

> —2 Peter 3:8–9

∾ According to these verses, why has Jesus not returned yet?

∾ According to these verses, what will happen to those who have not repented of their sin when Christ comes again?

❧ Today and Tomorrow ❧

TODAY: MY WORKS WILL BE JUDGED WHEN CHRIST APPEARS, WHETHER THEY ARE OF GOLD OR STRAW.

TOMORROW: I WILL ASK THE LORD TO TEACH ME HOW TO MAKE MY LIFE COUNT FOR ETERNITY.

❧ Notes and Prayer Requests: ❧

The Rapture and Other End-Time Events

ᴄᴧ In This Lesson ᴊᴧ

LEARNING: WHAT'S THE DIFFERENCE BETWEEN THE RAPTURE AND THE SECOND COMING?

GROWING: HOW CAN I PREPARE FOR THESE EVENTS?

A discussion about the Rapture of the church generally evokes two questions: *1. When does the Rapture occur with regard to the Great Tribulation? 2. Is the Rapture the same thing as the second coming of Christ?* We will deal specifically with these two questions in this lesson.

At the outset let me point out that the Bible has more than twenty times more verses about the Day of the Lord and the second coming of Christ than it does about the first coming of Jesus. A great deal has been written about the Great Tribulation and the Second Coming (Day of the Lord) in both the Old Testament and New Testament. Our purpose here is not to give a comprehensive account of end-time events, but to point out the distinctions among events and our need for preparation now so we will not experience God's wrath.

The Rapture and the Great Tribulation

A period of great tribulation is described in the Scriptures. This is not normal tribulation, which is a general term for trouble, trial, or sorrow and was described by Jesus when He said, "In the world you will have tribulation; but be of good cheer, I have overcome the world" (John 16:33). The Great Tribulation is a seven-year period of terrifying trouble on the earth. This period is first described by the prophet Daniel, and it is also described in vivid detail by John in the book of Revelation.

∞ The wrath of God ∞

During the Great Tribulation, the wrath of God will be poured out. The Great Tribulation is a time of judgment, and God has three main purposes for this period. First, the Lord will use the suffering of the Great Tribulation to call 144,000 people from Israel to be His witnesses on the earth to prepare for the Messiah's appearance. Second, the Lord will send witnesses to preach the gospel to the remaining Gentiles on the earth. Third, Satan will be given full opportunity to do his work through the Antichrist (also called the Beast) and the False Prophet, after which time Satan will be bound.

Opinions have been divided through the years concerning the timing of the Rapture with regard to the Great Tribulation. Some believe the Rapture will occur before the Tribulation, setting the starting point for the Tribulation. Some believe the Rapture occurs midway in the Tribulation (at a period of three and one half years), and some believe the Rapture occurs immediately before the end of the Tribulation and the second coming of Christ.

I believe the Rapture occurs before the Great Tribulation for two primary reasons. First, we are told repeatedly in the Scriptures to be ready for an unannounced, unpredictable Rapture that could occur at any moment. If the Rapture does not occur until after events of the Great Tribulation begin, the imminence and surprise element of the Rapture are negated.

Second, we are never told in Scripture that Christians will experience the wrath of God that is designated for nonbelievers. The Great Tribulation is a time of tremendous woes that encompass the entire earth. Furthermore, there is no mention of the church in the various manifestations of God's wrath described in Revelation from chapters four onward.

There are those who believe Christians will somehow be cleansed of sin and made more holy by the events of the Great Tribulation. Throughout the New Testament there is no means by which a person is cleansed from sin other than through the shed blood of Jesus. Suffering does not cleanse us. Our acceptance of Jesus' death on our behalf and the forgiveness offered by God the Father through our belief in Jesus bring us to the point where the Holy Spirit cleanses us. Events and circumstances do not cleanse or make us holy. Only God does that divine spiritual work in our lives.

Finally, there would be little reason for Paul to tell the church repeatedly to "comfort one another" with the truth of the Rapture if the church was going to experience the Great Tribulation. There will be little reason for hope or comfort during those frightful, terrible years.

> And there shall be a time of trouble, such as never was since there was a nation, even to that time. And at that time your people shall be delivered, every one who is found written in the book. And many of those who sleep in the dust of the earth shall awake, some to everlasting life, some to shame and everlasting contempt.
>
> —Daniel 12:1–2

What does it mean to be "found written in the book"? What book is this referring to? How does a person get his name written there?

What people will awaken to everlasting life? What people will receive everlasting contempt? Which group are you in?

The Rapture and the Second Coming

The Second Coming of Christ is also called the Day of the Lord in the Scriptures. This is a time of judgment for those remaining on the earth during the Great Tribulation and for those who have died without accepting Jesus as their Savior. The Rapture and the Second Coming differ in these distinct ways:

❧ The Rapture is for all believers; the Second Coming involves the elect who have endured to the end of the Great Tribulation (1 Thess. 4:16–17; Matt. 24:31).

❧ The Rapture results in believers joining together with the Lord in the air; at the Second Coming, the Lord comes to earth to set up His earthly reign (1 Thess. 4:17; Matt. 25:31–34).

❧ At the Second Coming the nations of the earth are judged, and the sheep are separated from the goats (Matt. 25:31–33; Zech. 14).

❧ The Rapture is imminent—it could happen at any time; the Second Coming follows a series of predicted events (Matt. 24).

❧ There is no mention of Satan at the Rapture; at the time of the Second Coming, Satan is bound (Rev. 20:1).

❧ The Rapture is sudden, without warning, and is experienced only by believers; at the Second Coming every eye will see the Lord (Rev. 1:7).

❧ The Rapture will bring hope and comfort to the heart of the believer; the Second Coming is a time when the tribes of the earth will mourn (Rev. 1:7).

When the Son of Man comes in His glory, and all the holy angels with Him, then He will sit on the throne of His glory. All
the nations will be gathered before Him, and He will separate
them one from another, as a shepherd divides his sheep from
the goats. And He will set the sheep on His right hand, but the
goats on the left.

—Matthew 25:31–33

❧ Which event is described in these verses: the Second Coming or the Rapture? What is the difference between the two
events?

❧ Who is Jesus referring to as sheep? As goats? Which are
you?

104

∞ Fire and devastation ∞

The Day of the Lord is associated with fire and devastation. The prophet Joel wrote:

> A fire devours before them,
> And behind them a flame burns;
> The land is like the Garden of Eden before them,
> And behind them a desolate wilderness;
> Surely nothing shall escape them.

—Joel 2:3

The prophet Zephaniah gives this word of the Lord:

> "I will utterly consume everything
> From the face of the land,"
> Says the Lord;
> "I will consume man and beast;
> I will consume the birds of the heavens,
> The fish of the sea,
> And the stumbling blocks along with the wicked.
> I will cut off man from the face of the land,"
> Says the Lord.

—Zephaniah 1:2–3

This complete renovation of the earth establishes the environment in which the Lord will work to create a new heaven and a new earth for His millennial reign.

What of Christ's Followers During These Events?

What will those who have loved and served the Lord Jesus Christ be doing during these days of great tribulation and at the time of the judgment of the Second Coming? The Scriptures hold out the promise that we will be in praise before the throne of God. We will be crying,

> You are worthy, O Lord,
> To receive glory and honor and power;
> For You created all things,
> And by Your will they exist and were created.

—Revelation 4:11

We will be saying with a loud voice:

> Worthy is the Lamb who was slain
> To receive power and riches and wisdom,
> And strength and honor and glory and blessing!...
> Blessing and honor and glory and power
> Be to Him who sits on the throne,
> And to the Lamb, forever and ever!"

—Revelation 5:12–13

We can prepare for these days by increasing our praise and worship now! Praise is one thing we can do on earth that we will continue to do through all eternity. Read what the psalmist foretells as the role of the saints in judging the nations with the Lord Jesus Christ:

Let the saints be joyful in glory;
Let them sing aloud on their beds.
Let the high praises of God be in their mouth,
And a two-edged sword in their hand,
To execute vengeance on the nations,
And punishments on the peoples;
To bind their kings with chains,
And their nobles with fetters of iron;
To execute on them the written judgment—
This honor have all His saints.
Praise the LORD!

—Psalm 149:5–9

And there will be signs in the sun, in the moon, and in the stars; and on the earth distress of nations, with perplexity, the sea and the waves roaring; men's hearts failing them from fear and the expectation of those things which are coming on the earth, for the powers of the heavens will be shaken. Then they will see the Son of Man coming in a cloud with power and great glory.

—Luke 21:25–27

~ Imagine what it will be like on earth when these events come to pass. Describe how you would feel if you experienced them.

⛫ How will these events differ from the Rapture? How can a person avoid this terrible day?

⛫ Today and Tomorrow ⛫

TODAY: THOSE WHO HAVE ACCEPTED CHRIST WILL NEVER FACE GOD'S JUDGMENT.

TOMORROW: I WILL SPEND TIME THIS WEEK PRAISING THE LORD FOR HIS GRACE AND MERCY.

Lesson 10

The Three W's

❧ In This Lesson ☙

Learning: What does the second coming of Christ have to do with life here and now?

Growing: What does God want me to be doing in my life?

∞

Repeatedly throughout the Scriptures we find three admonitions given to us about the Lord's return:

1. Watch faithfully

2. Work diligently

3. Wait peacefully

We Are to Watch

The Lord said repeatedly that we are to watch for His coming because we do not know the day or hour of Christ's appearing (Matt. 24:42; 25:13; Mark 13:35). Jesus gave this specific instruction in Luke 21:36: "Watch therefore, and pray always that you may be counted worthy to escape all these things that will come to pass, and to stand before the Son of Man."

Prayer is not the only thing we are to be doing as we watch. We are to stand fast in the faith, with courage and strength (1 Cor. 16:13). We are to watch soberly, arming ourselves with faith and love and salvation (1 Thess. 5:8). As we watch, we are to be especially aware of false prophets; we are to discern the spirits and to reject all who do not confess that Jesus Christ has come in the flesh and is God (1 John 4:1–2; 2 Peter 2:1). Jesus spoke to John in a vision and gave this great promise to those who are watchful: "Behold, I am coming as a thief. Blessed is he who watches, and keeps his garments, lest he walk naked and they see his shame" (Rev. 16:15).

> Watch, stand fast in the faith, be brave, be strong. Let all that you do be done with love.
>
> —1 Corinthians 16:13–14

❧ What does it mean to "stand fast in the faith"? Why is this important as you prepare for Christ's return?

❧ Why are we called to be brave and strong? In what ways are courage and strength needed in the Christian life?

110

We Are to Work

Why does Jesus leave us here on the earth after we are saved? Because we still have work to do! That work is twofold: evangelism and conformity to Christ. These two areas of work are not sequential; they are to be simultaneous.

∞ Evangelism ∞

Our first work is winning souls. We are to be the Lord's witnesses, telling of the love of God and of Jesus Christ's atoning death for our sin. We are to testify about what the Lord has done in our own lives, through our words and through the example of our lives. As long as there is a soul on earth who hasn't heard the gospel of Christ, we have work to do!

> But sanctify the Lord God in your hearts, and always be ready to give a defense to everyone who asks you a reason for the hope that is in you, with meekness and fear.
>
> —1 Peter 3:15

✍ What is the "hope that is in you"? What would you say to someone who asked you why you had such a hope?

❧ Why are meekness and fear important in evangelism? What are we to be afraid of? How will these things help to spread the gospel?

❧ Conformity to Christ ❧

Our second area for work is within ourselves: we are to grow spiritually in ever-increasing intimacy with the Lord. None of us is fully living up to our spiritual potential. We all have room to grow. The more we look at the life of Jesus Christ and experience His love, the more we will see places in our own lives where we are unlike Him. It is in those areas where we are not like Christ that we must become conformed to His likeness. Our minds must be renewed (Rom. 12:2). Our inner hurts and emotions must be healed. We must grow in our spiritual discernment and in the wisdom of God. Our faith must be strengthened and used so that our prayers and our actions are effective in building up the Lord's kingdom.

As we are conformed to the likeness of Christ and brought to maturity in Christ, we will increasingly find ourselves being used to build up others. Our conformity as individuals is part of the greater conformity of the entire church to be the living, active body of Christ on the earth. (See the In-Touch Bible study *Pursuing a Deeper Faith*.)

I beseech you therefore, brethren, by the mercies of God, that you present your bodies a living sacrifice, holy, acceptable to God, which is your reasonable service. And do not be conformed to this world, but be transformed by the renewing of your mind, that you may prove what is that good and acceptable and perfect will of God.

—Romans 12:1–2

🔖 What does it mean to be "conformed to this world"? How does this happen?

🔖 How does a person renew his mind? Why is this process necessary to understand the will of God?

We Are to Wait in Peace

Waiting isn't easy for many people. Impatience is often manifested by frustration. Waiting can also cause a buildup of fear in some people; the longer something doesn't happen, the more they imagine what *might* happen. Once we begin to imagine what might happen, fear is only a step away.

The angels spoke peace to the earth at Jesus' first coming (Luke 2:14). More than four hundred times in the Scriptures, the Lord says that we are not to fear but to have peace. The prophet Isaiah referred to Jesus as the Prince of Peace (Isa. 9:6). Throughout His ministry the Lord Jesus spoke peace: to a woman with an issue of blood He said, "Go in peace"; to a stormy sea He said, "Peace be still"; and to His disciples He said, "My peace I give you." The Lord calls us to peace as we await His return.

Apart from Jesus, there is no peace—not within a human heart and not among human beings or nations. With Jesus we can experience peace that passes our rational minds and settles deep within (Phil. 4:7). It is peace we are to seek and peace we are to find as we await the Lord's return.

Peace I leave with you, My peace I give to you; not as the world gives do I give to you. Let not your heart be troubled, neither let it be afraid.

—John 14:27

114

🔊 What sort of peace does the world offer? How is it different from the peace of God?

🔊 Why did Jesus command us not to permit our hearts to be troubled or afraid? How is this done? How can you deliberately choose not to fear?

What Is Your Answer?

When the Lord comes, will He find you among those who love Him and call Him Savior and Lord? Will He find you doing what He has commanded you to do? Will He find you eager to see Him? Will He find you ready for His appearing? When the Lord calls with a shout from heaven, will you instantly rise to be with Him? When the Lord appears in the clouds, will your heart rejoice with exceedingly great joy?

You have it within your will to answer these questions. How will you choose to respond to the Lord's challenges upon your life? The fact is, He is coming again!

> But let us who are of the day be sober, putting on the breastplate of faith and love, and as a helmet the hope of salvation. For God did not appoint us to wrath, but to obtain salvation through our Lord Jesus Christ, who died for us, that whether we wake or sleep, we should live together with Him.
>
> —1 Thessalonians 5:8–10

In what ways do faith and love work like a breastplate? How is the hope of salvation like a helmet?

ᕼ Why does Paul use these military metaphors to describe the Christian life? How can these things prepare us for Christ's return?

ᕼ Today and Tomorrow ᕲ

TODAY: GOD WANTS ME TO BECOME CONFORMED TO THE IMAGE OF CHRIST.

TOMORROW: I WILL LIVE MY LIFE EACH DAY IN THE EAGER EXPECTATION OF HIS IMMINENT RETURN.

Notes and Prayer Requests:

∞ **Notes and Prayer Requests:** ∞

⚭ Notes and Prayer Requests: ⚭

∞ **Notes and Prayer Requests:** ∞

◦∞◦ Notes and Prayer Requests: ◦∞◦

Notes and Prayer Requests:

∝ **Notes and Prayer Requests:** ∝

Printed in the USA
CPSIA information can be obtained
at www.ICGtesting.com
JSHW011028140724
66378JS00006B/41